SCHIRMER'S LIBRARY OF MUSICAL CLASSICS

Vol. 825

ROBERT SCHUMANN

Op. 85

Twelve
Four-Hand Piano-Pieces

For Large and Small Children

Edited and Fingered by

LOUIS OESTERLE

G. SCHIRMER, Inc.

DISTRIBUTED BY

HAL•LEONARD®
CORPORATION

7777 W. BLUEMOUND RD. P.O. BOX 13819 MILWAUKEE, WI 53213

INDEX

Twelve Four-hand Piano-pieces
For Large and Small Children.

Geburtstagsmarsch.
Birthday-March.

Robert Schumann, Op. 85.
Composed in 1849.

Twelve Four-hand Piano-pieces

For Large and Small Children.

Geburtstagsmarsch.
Birthday-March.

Robert Schumann, Op. 85.
Composed in 1849.

1. Primo.

Bärentanz.
Bear Dance.

Bärentanz.
Bear Dance.

Gartenmelodie.
Garden Melody.

3.

Gartenmelodie.
Garden Melody.

Beim Kränzewinden.
Twining Wreaths.

Nicht zu schnell.
Moderato. (♩ = 96)

4.

Beim Kränzewinden.
Twining Wreaths.

10

(a) This melody-note leads to g in the *primo* part.

Kroatenmarsch.

Croatian March.

Kroatenmarsch.
Croatian March.

Nach und nach schwächer
poco a poco dim.

Immer schwächer und schwächer

sempre poco a poco dim.

Trauer.
Mourning.

Nicht schnell.
Moderato. (♩ = 63)

6.

Trauer.
Mourning.

Turniermarsch.
Tournament March.

Sehr kräftig.
Molto pesante.

7.

Turniermarsch.
Tournament March.

Reigen.
Circle Dance.

8.

Reigen.
Circle Dance.

29

Am Springbrunnen.
By the Fountain.

So schnell wie möglich.
Presto possibile.

9.

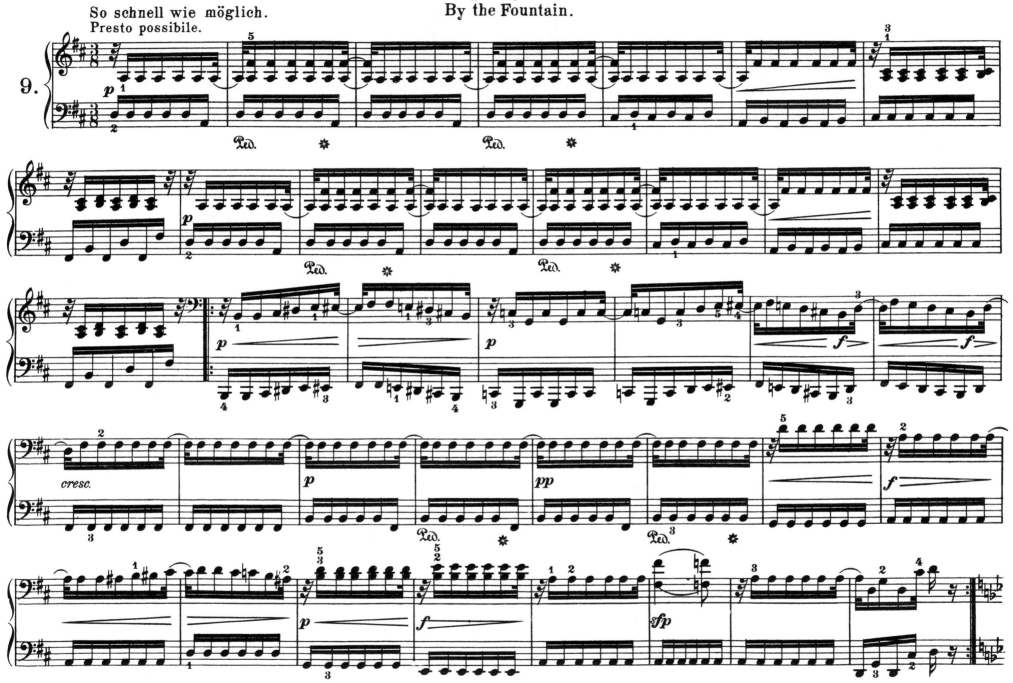

Am Springbrunnen.
By the Fountain.

So schnell wie möglich.
Presto possibile.

9.

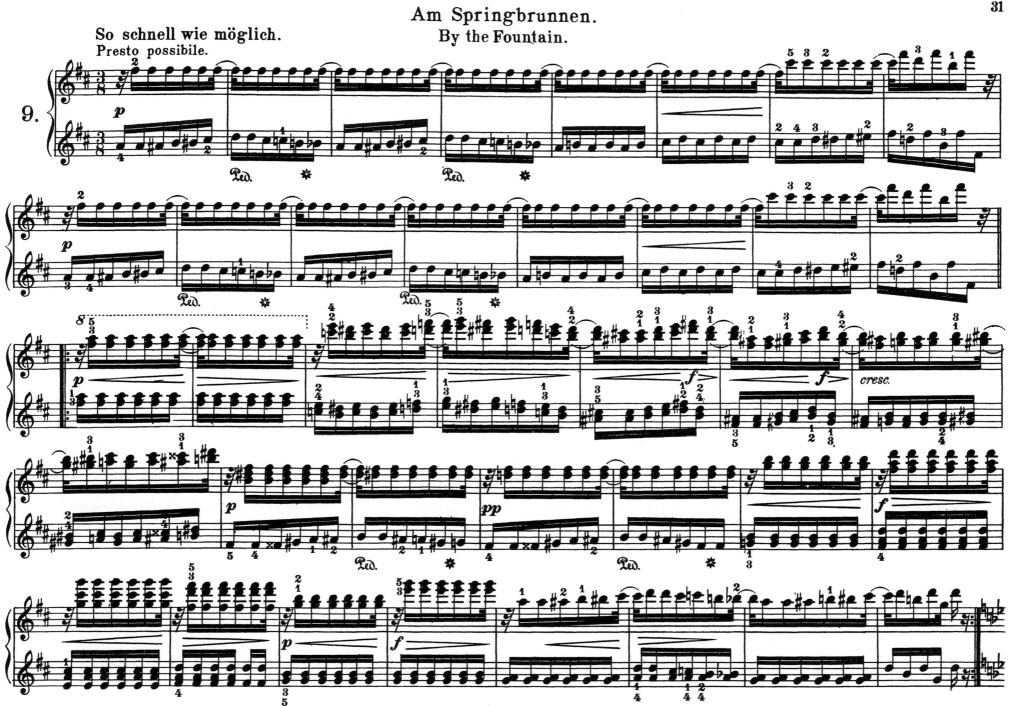

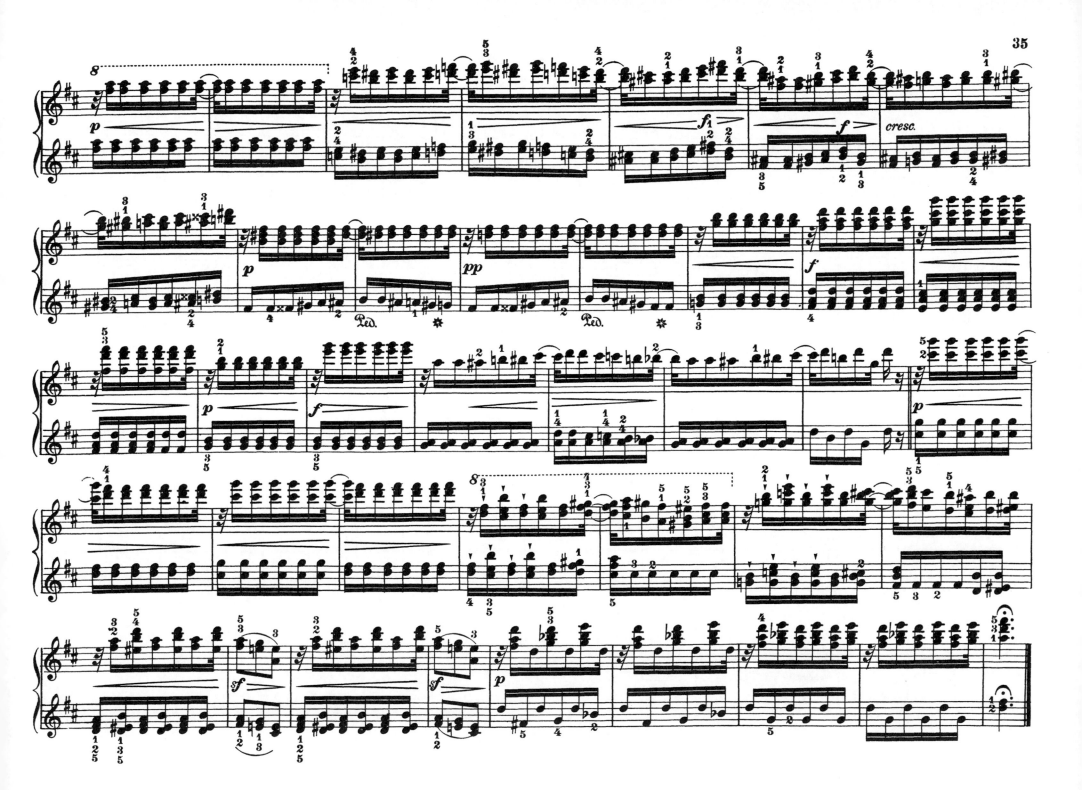

Versteckens.
Hide-and-go-seek.

Versteckens.
Hide-and-go-seek.

Gespenstermärchen.
Ghost-stories.

Gespenstermärchen.
Ghost-stories.

Abendlied.
Evening Song.

Ausdrucksvoll und sehr gehalten.
Espressivo e molto sostenuto. ($\bullet$=52)

Abendlied.
Evening Song

Fine.